Dedicated to my mom, the first strong
Black woman in my life. —CRS

To all the Black girls out there, you are beautiful,
you are brave, you are unstoppable. And to all the
grownups who needed a Bessie when young, it's
never too late to find your courage. —CK

Text copyright © 2022 by Charles R. Smith Jr.
Illustrations copyright © 2022 by Charlot Kristensen

Library of Congress Cataloging-in-Publication Data Available

ISBN 978-1-338-75247-2

10 9 8 7 6 5 4 3 2 1   22 23 24 25 26

Printed in China   38
First edition, September 2022

Book design by Sarah Dvojack
Art direction by Brian LaRossa

The text type was set in Ruluko. The display type was set in KG From Where You Are.

Bessie the Motorcycle QUEEN

Written by
Charles R. Smith Jr.

Illustrated by
Charlot Kristensen

ORCHARD BOOKS / NEW YORK

Gotta Get Gas Money

Laddiieeees and gentlemennnn,
boyyyyyssss and girrrrlllllssss,
step right up
to witness
the challenge of all challenges,
the thrill of all thrills,
the monstrous,
the treacherous

WALLLLL OF DEATHHHH,

standing twenty feet high
and forty feet wiiiiide!

Who would dare
take on such a challenge?

Bessie,
the Motorcycle Queen,
that's who.

There she goes,
circling,
circling,
faster
and faster,
reaching speeds
up to sixty miles per hour.

VROOOOOM-VROOOOOM
VROOOOOOOOOOMMMMM

See Bessie ride
with no hands to steer.
See Bessie ride
sidesaddle with no fear.
And if you want to see more,
chant, "Go, Bessie, go,"
then come meet the Queen
after the show.

Meet

The folks, they lined up
to meet the Motorcycle Queen,
seated sidesaddle
on her motorbike machine,
still wearing her helmet
with her face unseen.

the Queen

Bessie slung her jacket
over her back,
reached under her chin
and undid her strap,
slid off her helmet
with style and grace,
then stunned the crowd
with her hidden brown face.

See,
it was the year
1929
and faces of color
weren't treated kind,
all because
of color separation,
due to a law
called segregation.

But folks smiled at Bessie,
wanting to know
Bessie's life story
show after show.

Where'd you learn to ride like that?

How old are you?

How long you been riding?

Where do you live?

Where you going?

Show after show,
the questions never changed,
so Bessie told her story
again and again.

Bessie Gets a Bike

Bessie began riding
at the age of sixteen,
when a birthday gift
appeared like a dream.
A motorbike she rode
day after day,
teaching herself
until she rode away.

Yeah, Bessie left Boston
behind as she rolled,
and at nineteen years old,
her home was the road.

But when it came to one question,
the answer constantly changed:
"Where you going?"
because it was never the same.

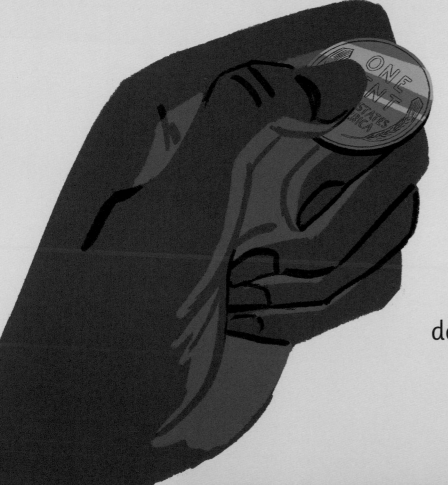

See, Bessie had a map
and Bessie had a penny,
and a flip of that penny
determined Bessie's next journey.

MISSI

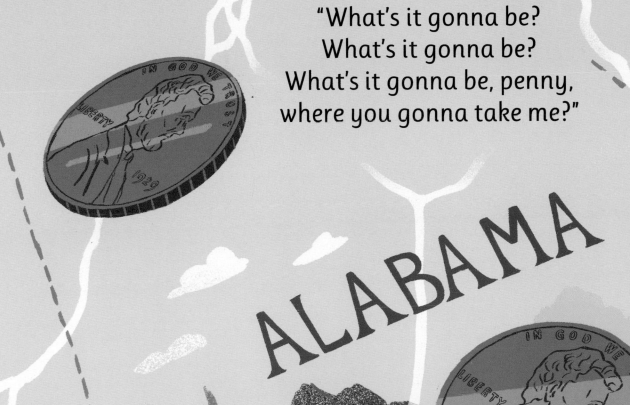

"What's it gonna be?
What's it gonna be?
What's it gonna be, penny,
where you gonna take me?"

"Where the Penny Takes Me"

A young Black woman,
alone but not lonely.
Bessie's best friend was the road,
wide open and calling.

Rolling over bridges,
rolling across mountains,
mile after mile
Bessie kept on rolling.

Over highways and dirt roads,
Bessie rolled to new places,
through big cities and small towns,
meeting new faces,
some smiling
some curious
mostly friendly
mostly gracious.

But as Bessie rolled south,
those friendly, smiling faces
became angry faces,
and signs soon appeared
forbidding Bessie places.

But Bessie just rolled,
rolled past each sign.
Bessie **VROOM-VROOOOMED**
to leave Jim Crow behind,
because Bessie's dark face
in unfamiliar places
could easily lead to chases
by angry mobs of racists.

Stone Mountain, Georgia

Wearing white sheets
here they come
here they come.
In the rearview getting bigger
here they come
here they come.

A pickup truck full of men
here they come
here they come.

Full of screaming, angry men
here they come
here they come.

Getting closer
going faster
here they come
here they come.

Screaming
shouting
honking
here they come
here they come.

Barreling down on Bessie
here they come
here they come
but they'd never catch Bessie,
'cause Bessie would go **go go**

FAST

with the throttle revved open
burning up gas.

VROOM-VROOM

VROOOOOOOOM

Bessie took off with a thrust,
leaving white sheets behind
in a dirty cloud of dust!

Pit Stop

Bessie burned through her gas
and needed a pit stop
but where could she go,
where could she flop?

GAS

Bessie's brown face
wasn't welcome in the South,
so Bessie relied
on word of mouth
for where to get gas,
where to sleep for the night,
but when there were no rooms,
Bessie slept on her bike.

Her jacket became her pillow,
her seat became her bed,
and Bessie slept beneath a blanket
of stars overhead.
When the rising sun
warmed Bessie's face,
she pulled out her penny,
ready to roll to a new place.

"What's it gonna be, penny, where you gonna take me next?"

IN GOD WE TRUST
LIBERTY 1929

ARIZONA

With a kick-start and a **VROOOOM**, Bessie pointed her wheels west.

The Unforgiving Road

Flat tires and misfires
never caused Bessie panic
'cause miles on the road
taught Bessie to be her own mechanic.

But the side of the road
was a dangerous place to be
for a Black woman, because cars
would often try to hit Bessie.

But Bessie stayed focused,
focused on the task
of fixing her bike
as cars rode past.

RACING CONTEST

Back on the road
Bessie soon needed gas,
and Bessie needed food,
so Bessie needed cash.

Races vs. Racists

Off to the races,
the prize-money races,
Bessie entered
and won
on a regular basis,
kicking up dust
in left-behind faces.

But sometimes those faces
became angry faces
when Bessie's brown face
kept winning races,
so Bessie couldn't collect
her prize in some places.

But Bessie didn't care,
she knew she still won,
Bessie **VROOOM-VROOOMED** west
following the sun.

Where to Next?

Rolling
rolling
rolling west
to the canyons of Arizona,
then where to next?

Maybe the mountains in Montana?
Maybe the coast of California?
Maybe back to Boston?
Maybe the lakes of Minnesota?

Bessie didn't care
because Bessie was free.
The Motorcycle Queen lived her life
at the flip of a penny.

Bessie's Story

I came across the story of Bessie Stringfield one cold February day while scrolling through social media. February is Black History Month, and someone had posted a very short video about her as "someone you should know." The video was only about ninety seconds long, but when it was over, I was fascinated with this adventurous young Black woman and wanted to learn more.

Not much was written about Bessie, and what was written often came from the same source, a motorcycle-riding journalist by the name of Ann Ferrar. The two became friends through a shared love of riding, and Ann interviewed Bessie to share her story. When Bessie was inducted into the American Motorcyclist Association Hall of Fame, Ferrar wrote a short biography that guided me early in my research.

As I continued my research, months turned into years, and details of Bessie's story began to change. Originally, I learned that she was born Betsy Lenora Ellis, but I later learned she was born Bessie Beatrice White. I also learned she was born in 1911. Or 1912. Or 1918. And that she was born in Jamaica. Or was it the American South? Or Massachusetts? Bessie spun some tall tales, so it was hard to know the true details of her life. But one thing that remained consistently true was Bessie's adventures of riding a motorcycle across the country at a young age — specifically, her "penny-flip trips." So that's what I focused on.

Traveling across the United States in the late 1920s through the early 1930s could be difficult for Black people, especially a lone Black woman on a motorcycle. So I wanted to show the challenges that Bessie faced. She needed to find places to sleep, eat, and get gas that served Black people. This was not always easy. But to Bessie, that was part of the adventure.

After her cross-country travels, Bessie rode her motorcycle for the US Army during WWII as a dispatch rider. She carried classified documents between American military bases and was the only woman in an all-Black unit. Bessie had the respect of every rider due to her skill, fearlessness, and positive attitude.

Bessie later made her home near Miami, Florida, where she earned her license as a practical nurse. To connect with other riders, she founded the Iron Horse Motorcycle Club. Every year she led a parade on her Harley Davidson and was known for sharing the steering duties with her two poodles. She owned twenty-seven Harleys over her lifetime.

Bessie passed away in 1993, having lived a free-spirited life filled with tall tales and wild adventures. I hope her story inspires you to pursue your own adventures.

Bibliography

BOOKS

Ferrar, Ann. *Hear Me Roar: Women, Motorcycles and the Rapture of the Road.* Crown Trade Paperbacks/Random House, 1996.

Gill, Joel Christian. *Bessie Stringfield: Tales of the Talented Tenth.* Fulcrum Publishing, 2016.

ONLINE ARTICLES

Ferrar, Ann. "Bessie Stringfield, Southern Distance Rider." American Motorcyclist Association Hall of Fame, 2002, excerpted by the National Motorcycle Museum. www.nationalmcmuseum.org/featured-articles/bessie-stringfield-southern-distance-rider/.

Ferrar, Ann. "Bessie Stringfield: The First Stories of a Courageous Life (Part 1)." www.bessiestringfieldbook.com."

Stewart, Nikita. "Overlooked No More: Bessie B. Stringfield, the 'Motorcycle Queen of Miami.'" *New York Times*, April 4, 2018. www.nytimes.com/2018/04/04/obituaries/overlooked-bessie-stringfield.html.